Glitter

Suretha Badenhorst

Presentation by *BookLeaf Publishing*

Web: www.bookleafpub.com

E-mail: info@bookleafpub.com

ISBN: 978-93-95755-65-8

First edition 2022

To Mum and Dad

For always supporting my creative endeavours, and praying for me when I needed it most

May you both be richly blessed, in Jesus name - Numbers 6:24-26

Thanks for everything

Circle Of Life

If ever I want to be something, it would be a
soldier.
A big strong soldier who saves the world from
war.

If ever I want to be something, it would be a
nurse.
A nurse dressed in green, who saves the soldiers
from death by sewing up their bad wounds.

If ever I want to be something, it would be a
doctor.
A friendly, smart doctor who could instruct his
nurses on how to operate.

If ever I want to be something, it would be a
teacher.
A teacher to teach doctors how to operate so one
day they could save a life.

If ever I want to be something, it would be a
mother.
A mother to have a child. A big strong, child
who would become a soldier.

(Age 10 - 2002)

Spectrum Reflections

Like a rainbow is my mind
Full of colours a million and one,
Some are YELLOW and kind,
But others are RED like the setting sun;

Full of rage and of destruction -
A huge mean wave crashing on me.
I am angered by today's corruption
Of minds for money - Why? I simply cannot see.

Yet, I am calmed like the GREEN grass,
Blowing in the breeze,
When I tell myself 'Even this will pass'
And so I am at ease.

Still, I feel sad for the living Earth
That we are cutting down, killing its beauty
These actions are neglecting it's worth;
I think it should be all of humanity's duty

To paint the GREY skies BLUE once more,
To lessen the factory smoke,
To plant more trees and help the poor,
And to live forever in hope…

My thoughts are blank, WHITE and confusing,
As I wonder what will happen if we continue to
kill:
If we continue this abusing,
The future seems BLACK

                        and

                             still.

PURPLE: The deep contemplation
As I wonder in what kind of place
I will have to raise my children

  Is there any hope for the human race?

(Age 12- 2004 - This was the first poem Suretha
entered into a contest. It won first place.)

Growing Up

It began with a cry
And a rush of cold air
It was my first breath
I am the child mum had to bear
It began on April 30th
And although I was only small
The doctors told mum and dad
One day I would be tall.

It was followed by the terrible twos
And threes, and fours, and fives
Something that forever would
Change my parents lives
But it would also change mine
As many things I learnt
Like not to touch something hot
Or else you would get burnt

It came then to childhood
And first days of school
Of learning all my manners
Of using words like 'cool'
And if my parents thought that then
My antics were quite strange
They didn't know what they were in for

When I became: teenaged!

And yes that came
That was next
And all my friends
I had to text
On my new mobile
Which was the latest invention
And being good at the time
Was not of my intention
(Was that why I was always in detention?)

(A work in progress from ages 12 - 13, 2004 -
2005)

Longing

I miss you in my highs
I miss you in my lows
I miss your voice; the goodbyes and hellos

I miss you in the morning
I miss you in the night
I miss your smile; my darkness's light

I miss you in my arms
I miss you in the phone
I miss your very presence; now I am alone

I missed you today
I'll miss you tomorrow too

I miss you

Reject Their Perfect

This poem aims to challenge your perceived
normality
Why do we let duplicates crowd reality?

Why do we need mirrors to tell us who we are?
We are not defined by our clothes, house, or car

What makes "this thing" better than "that"?
Trying to keep up like an acrobats act

Trendy is a thief stealing individuality
Your version of "cool" reveals your personality

Break through the mask of social conformity
Examine the simplicity of who you were born to
be

See

Maybe I'm man made, but I'm not artificial
Being someone's copy is not beneficial

Rebuke the need to compare, blend in with the
crowd

To win or lose by their standards shouldn't make
you proud

If society determines every form of your
expression
All their adoration will leave an empty
impression

It's not who you are that determines success
It's who you feel worthy of being -

YOU'RE NOT LESS!

Measure up to YOUR standards, take back the
control
You don't need to find yourself in order to be
whole

Deep inside you always knew: your words, your
taste, your style
Embrace your persona, stop living in denial

And smile!

Fried Rice

Happiness! It has no price
Yet this is the advertisement for fried rice

Ice ice baby, "good times", "fun ahead"
Perspectives biggest untruth - mind frozen like lead

It happens with dope, amphetamines, pills
Always forking out with expectation of thrills

Here is the truth, right here in this poem:
Anger engulfs during scattered unknown

Entering mental confusion
Viewing through an illusion

Questioning pointless existence
Next hit your only resistance

Right and wrong in misconstrue
Completely forgetting who really is you

Drugs take you when you take them
Into Hell never back again

Depression looming
Darkness consuming

Prospect of "joy" seeming attractive
Believing you NEED that psychoactive

Always longing to "obtain clear thought"
A twisted "reality" you have bought

Without; only an empty feeling
Heart pounding fast as the fan on the ceiling

Shaking and sweating and "hearing them laugh"
Only no one is there, tis a dark lonely path

When you have some everyone hangs like flies
But no one sticks by once "it's done" is realised

See, real relationships have now all been lost
You've sold your soul at what cost?

High's Of High

The chasing
The waiting
The begging, debating
The calling and texting
The ticking

Of the pocket and the clock

Just to get a rock
Just to get a stick
Just to get a pill
Just to get a sip
Whatever your thrill

Detachment from time
Reality too
Really who are you?
No, really, WHO ARE YOU?

No money no food
Bills overdue
No clue what to do
Wanting anything
Needing something
Having nothing

Just to "see you through"

Teeth a rot
What have you got?
The fights
The stress
Hair a mess
NEED to obtain
What's to gain?

Happy Sad
Excited Mad
Feeling good, then feeling bad

Mood swings
Pawned rings
All sorts of pawned things

Can't get on? Oh misery
Is this your only destiny?

To chase
To score
To get some more
To fail
To cry for what you cannot buy
Why do you care so much? Oh why!

Destroying friendships

Family pushed aside
Never have time
Taking up crime
Stealing necessities to survive
Hope of normal life no sight to your eyes

Concerning onlookers
Zero care
Especially when drugs are there
You don't share
In dirty underwear
House chores not done
But you're having fun

Right?

"This Will Be My Last"

Always, forever, 'this will be my last'
Quitting, thoughtlessly aside cast
When asked 'Would you like some', when
passed The Pipe
'Why not, tis my last, it'll be alright'

One blink later, many years are gone
Span of time didn't feel very long
Never felt right, neither quite wrong
All along 'one last time' urging you on

Previous 'last time' left wanting more
Whether free or putting out savings to score
Priorities blurred, mind absurd
Feeling as free as a caged bird

Best feeling was always experience the first
Never can quench an always increasing thirst
Like seeking out fictitious coins at the rainbows
finish
Same's chasing this feeling which every use
does diminish

Worth of time spent, questionable now
A logical asking overlooked somehow

Hours and dollars, up in smoke, ticked away
Thinking 'Just one last puff, it'll be okay'

Repetitive thinking 'next time I'll say no
I'm too young, it's too soon, too much fun to let
go
Tomorrow todays matters can matter
Today this brain may scatter and patter'

Unexpectedly soon reality says "Wait!"
Unprepared for deaths bed, realization too late
A life spent consumed in a justifying state
Only a lack of dedication remains to
contemplate

Many blank moment, nothing to recall
Were those 'last times' worth it at all
Hours evaporated, present and past
Lifespan reduction realised at last

Forever forward going clock, to rewind is to
dream
Perhaps those 'last times' weren't all they had
seemed
Too few recollections, plans never seen through
A denied addiction forever controlled you!

Could I?

I've walked through Oz
Down a yellow brick road
Wondering what stories it held, untold

Who paved it and why, and when, and how
Could I click my heels and go home, somehow?

I've swam like a mermaid
Through the deep sea
And wondered how life on the surface might be

Is there someone up there worth changing for
Could I hold my breath long enough to reach the
shore?

I've wandered castle walls
Trapped there by a beast
Where a chipped chattering cup joined me for a
feast

Would this curse end with love true as they say
Could I see those I missed again someday?

I was lost from The Rock
Until a baboon old and wise
Hit me on the head and made me realise

Home longed for me, this truth set me free
Could I reclaim my pride and who I was born to
be?

Finding Alice

Come sweet Alice
Let's walk slow
Tell me of the places you wish to go
Of all the things you long to see
How your real wonderland would be

Come here Alice
Take a minute
Do you like that blue dress with white in it
What deep desires lie in your heart
Come, share your story, right from the start

Come now Alice
Please do tell
Of the Mad Hatter you knew so well
Why follow a rabbit down a deep hole
Is Queen of Hearts as bad as is told

Alice oh Alice
The things that you've seen
'Eat me' and 'Drink me' surely must take the cream
Or a playing cards pack painting white roses red
While a staunch little woman shouts "Off with their head!"

Walk now with me Alice
Tell me, were you scared
Afraid that you may get trapped down there
Did the Cheshire Cat have a smile very bright
Do you dream ever of Wonderland at night

Oh my Alice
If opportunity came
Would you think to visit Wonderland again
Was it a dream, a trick of the mind
Or was there sincerely a rabbit behind time
Would you invite someone else too
Or is this experience only for you

I must say Alice
You're famous you know
You could go any place you wish to go
Do anything you wish to do
Your future adventures depend only on...

You

Lost

Some abstract poetry:

Who are you?

You lost yourself
To this miserable existence
Nothing changes
You can't cycle through a day
Happy, content, accomplished.

You lost yourself
In the pursuit of brick walls that look like people
Words that take you to the past, not present
The smell of laundry powder and floor cleaner
Like that's what life's about.

You lost yourself
Between the could be's and maybe's
Someday's dreams
Hopes that like shattered glass
Still hurt.

You lost yourself
Inside the pills that numb
That drink that helps you sleep

Only to dream of the nightmare
You cannot escape.

See
You lost yourself, trying to find yourself
In a broken world of broken people
Trying to mend your broken pieces with broken
things

       When only God saves

Who are you?

The 2020 Reset

And somewhere in the midst of the silence,
caused by the chaos,
They found something they didn't know had
been missing all this time.

It was a peace, a tranquil realisation of what
TRULY matters.

Suddenly, the busy lifestyle, the constant scuttle
of an everyday society,
No longer seemed so appealing.

And they realised the voice inside had known
this all along.

The stress about the mess, being late, making
mistakes...
It was all frozen in this precious moment of
gifted time.

And it all made sense.

These moments. These days. They weren't made
to fly past;
One blurring into another, into another.

They were made to be felt.

Experienced deeply and slowly, like a love story
unfolding,
Giving deeper meaning to every breath we take.

They started writing again, feeling inspired.

Planting, painting, priorities changed.
They consumed all the time that wasn't there
before - slowly it began,

Instinctively; a natural occurrence.

And when they looked at how things used to be,
Yes everything WAS different.

But not the good kind of different.

The kind of different that took up space, and
time,
Consumed feelings and thoughts so that
everything was numb.

And this became clear in the pause.

All those years were a storm they were too numb
to feel, too blind to see.

And now that the veil had been lifted they hoped
it would never be put over -

Again.

Looking Glass

Grief and love share many features
Staring at eachother
Reflecting in the glass

Griefs face is a little longer
Yet it makes love a little stronger
And loves eyes are a little brighter
Making griefs burdens a little lighter
A little tighter, inadvertedly

But universally

Both have cried
Both have the other multiplied
Both in the human heart reside

Eternally

Addicted To Fruit

Inspired by the fruits of the Holy Spirit
(Galatians 5:22-23):

Once I was an addict

I chased the highs that brought me low
I chased the warmth but found the snow
I chased the drugs that won't let go
I chased the gossip I needn't know
I chased the fast and couldn't slow
I chased the love I couldn't show
Once I was an addict
An addict of the world

Now I am an addict

I walk in love to my fellow
I walk in peace deeply mellow
I walk in joy instead of woe
I walk in patience the road narrow
I walk in kindness that leaves a glow
I walk in faithfulness to sow
I walk in self control to grow

Because He paid a debt He didn't owe

He gave me joy for my sorrow
I will my praise on Him bestow
Jesus is worthy, my hero
His cross defeated every foe
Thank You Jesus for that victorious blow

Now I am addicted
Addicted to the fruit

Galatians 6:7-8
"Do not be deceived: God cannot be mocked. A
man reaps what he sows. The one who sows to
please his sinful nature, from that nature will
reap destruction; the one who sows to please the
Spirit, from the Spirit will reap eternal life."

Bite The Bullet

Inspired by idioms and oxymorons:

There is something to be said
About these wounds in my back
And weapons held by 'friends'

Familiar faces
Once bitten twice shy

Empty promises
Burn bridges

True lies
Speak for themselves

Take this with a pinch of salt:
'Anticipate no ferocity in a tame lion
Despite it's teeth'

Read between the lines
Yet keep in mind

There is light at the end of the tunnel
It is always darkest before the dawn

Prayer From A Heavy Heart

A poem I wrote, for those times one cries out
before God:

I am tired of the mind games
I am tired of the traps
I am tired of human chess pieces
"One step ahead", doing laps

I am tired of the fake friends
I am tired of the lies
I am tired beyond tired
I lay down, and close my eyes

While true rest evades me
I decide now is the time
I'm already in position
All set and all primed

I am ready to speak my heart out
To cast my cares on Him
My Lord of Lord's, My King of Kings
The knower of all things

As I begin to pour my worries
As one pours a cup of tea

The heaviness flows out and down
Then rises up like steam

My cries reach to the ears of God
They squeeze through Heaven's gate
To where He sit's upon the throne
Never early, never late

These words, they swirl inside my mouth
They almost burn my tongue
To think on these things was hard enough
To speak them, a smoking gun

As implied, the trigger has been pulled
A bitter stench, thick in the air
Yet it clears away quickly
When the Holy Spirit enters there

I can feel my peace returning
As I know it's in God's hand
And every evil scheme and plot
Will have the end that God has planned

The devil has no victory
In my mind, my soul, my heart
The Lord God has heard me from His throne
And healed my every part

- God bless -

Narrow Is The Way

Inspired by Matthew 7:13-14

Keep me on Your narrow road
Don't let me go astray
Keep me on Your narrow road
Show to me the way

Keep me on Your narrow road
With rod and staff direct
Keep me on Your narrow road
Guide, lead, and correct

Keep me on Your narrow road
Looking to Your Son
Keep me on Your narrow road
Speak to me "well done"

Keep me on Your narrow road
Oh God, if You don't
Keep me on Your narrow road
I won't make it, I won't

The Mirror

I used to look at Judas
A disloyal thieving liar
How could he betray Jesus?
Doesn't he deserve the fire?

Other times I observed Barabbas
Who in their right mind would let HIM go?
A murderer, a violent man
He had no good seeds to sow

And I've thought I know a Barabbas
A Judas I used to call friend
Someone who broke my heart deeply
A most painful wound to mend

But the closer I looked at these people
One thing becomes blatantly clear
When I look at Judas and Barabbas
I'm really staring into a mirror

Romans 3:23
We all have fallen short
In word, deed, and thought

Encore

This night I watch the stars
They dance above my head
A most marvelous concert
That keeps me from my bed

I play connect the dots
One bright spark to another
Imaginations pictures
That reality would smother

I see fireworks
They shoot across the sky
Stardust explosions
That dazzle and electrify

Oh to be a beam of light
A free feisty fire
Tonight I admire
A distant attire I desire

Letters From My Eyes

I'd like to share some exerts
Of letters from my eyes
Words rolled down from cheek to chin
Each unique in their advise

First, those too late letters
A silent guilt that eats the soul
A longing to return
What I have from others stole

"For every unspoken thank you
Every cruel word that broke your heart
Every action that made me despicable
Sorry is meaningless, but, I truly art"

Now one for the old flames
Eyes water quenched each fire
Their amends returned to sender
No longer my hearts desire

"This presently heavy burden
Of goodbye tears lingers
Like unwanted sticky cobwebs
On a feather dusters fingers"

This I wrote a dear friend
They stuck by in a time of need
Support opened eyes floodgates
And encouraged me to succeed

"And on those days that feel so long
They drag on and on, it's hard to be strong
I'll read your message and remember there
Are others who understand and also care"

Next a simple postcard
Handwritten, sent from afar
Though this is all that remains of you
It brings healing to deaths scar

"You are so very special
I miss you every day
I love you always, forever
You are my light when skies are grey"

Last, I'll share this letter
I addressed it to myself
It lived inside my wallet
To remind me of my health

"Strength is persevering
You've put many lives on hold
Losing and finding are difficult
So look forward, self controlled"

There are many different letters
Transferred from my eyes
Pieces of life's story
Put together to make me wise

One day I'll read back through them
Bitter and precious libraries
Collected by my eyes
To form life's realities

Reason To Smile

"Life is beautiful, wild and free," She once said
to me.

"What is it that makes it so?" I encouraged her to
show.

"The limitless simplicity of endless possibility,"
She happily sighed and smiled at me.